THE RELIC OF KAAL BHAVAN

THE HIDDEN LEGACY

AKSHAT THAPA

To my parents, for their unwavering support and encouragement. To my teachers, for igniting my passion for storytelling. And to every reader, for embarking on this journey with me. This book is for you.

Contents

Foreword — vii

Preface — ix

Acknowledgements — xi

Prologue — xiii

1. Whispers Of The Past — 1

2. The Guardian's Warning — 13

3. The Hidden Chamber — 19

4. Whispers In The Shadows — 25

5. Echoes Of The Past — 31

6. Shadows In The Night — 37

7. The Price Of Knowledge — 43

8. The Final Confrontation — 48

Foreword

Writing "The Relic of Kaal Bhavan" has been a journey filled with discovery, emotion, and immense dedication. As a twelfth-grade student, I embarked on this literary adventure driven by my fascination with mythology and the mysteries that lie within. This story is not just about the characters and their trials, but a reflection of the universal struggle between light and darkness, both within and around us.

This book wouldn't have been possible without the guidance and support of my family, friends, and teachers. Their belief in my vision gave me the courage to bring this tale to life. I hope that as you turn the pages, you are transported into the world of Kaal Bhavan and experience the suspense, the sacrifice, and the triumphs of its characters.

Thank you for joining me on this journey. May the story of Kaal Bhavan resonate with you and leave a lasting impression.

akshat thapa

FOREWORD

Preface

"The Relic of Kaal Bhavan" began as a simple idea, sparked by my fascination with ancient myths and the supernatural. As a twelfth-grade student, I found myself drawn to the untold stories and hidden histories that lie beneath the surface of our everyday world. The concept of Kaal Bhavan, a mansion steeped in mystery and darkness, took root in my imagination and grew into the intricate tale you now hold in your hands.

Writing this book has been both challenging and rewarding. It required delving deep into the realms of myth and legend, exploring the complexities of human nature, and confronting the themes of fear, sacrifice, and redemption. The characters in this story are not just figments of my imagination; they are reflections of the struggles and triumphs that we all experience.

Throughout this journey, I have been supported by a wonderful network of family, friends, and mentors. Their encouragement has been invaluable, and their belief in my vision has kept me motivated.

This preface is an invitation to step into the world of Kaal Bhavan, to uncover its secrets, and to join Rajiv, Ananya, and Professor Mehta as they navigate the darkness and strive for light. I hope that this story captivates you, challenges you, and ultimately leaves you with a sense of wonder and possibility.

Thank you for embarking on this adventure with me.

Acknowledgements

Writing "The Relic of Kaal Bhavan" has been an incredible journey, and it would not have been possible without the support and encouragement of many people.

First and foremost, I would like to thank my family for their unwavering belief in me. Their constant support and understanding have been my foundation throughout this process.

I am deeply grateful to my friends who have patiently listened to my ideas, offered invaluable feedback, and encouraged me to keep going, even when the path seemed difficult.

A special thank you to my teachers and mentors who have inspired me to push the boundaries of my creativity and to believe in the power of storytelling. Your guidance has been instrumental in shaping this book.

I would also like to acknowledge my beta readers, whose keen eyes and thoughtful critiques have helped refine this story. Your contributions have been essential in bringing Kaal Bhavan to life.

Finally, to all the readers who pick up this book, thank you for your curiosity and for taking the time to delve into the world I have created. Your support means everything to me, and I hope this story resonates with you as much as it has with me.

Akshat Thapa

Prologue

In the heart of a remote village, where time seemed to stand still, stood an ancient mansion known as Kaal Bhavan. For generations, it loomed as a silent sentinel, casting long, foreboding shadows over the village. Locals whispered tales of its dark history, of curses and spirits that lingered within its walls. Few dared to venture near, and those who did seldom returned with their sanity intact.

Centuries ago, Kaal Bhavan was a place of grandeur and prosperity. It was home to a powerful dynasty that ruled with wisdom and strength. However, an unspoken darkness lurked beneath the surface, a relic of unimaginable power that demanded a terrible price. As the years passed, the once-vibrant mansion fell into decay, and the whispers of its cursed legacy grew louder.

Rajiv, a curious and determined young man, found himself drawn to the mysteries of Kaal Bhavan. Despite the warnings and the palpable fear that surrounded the mansion, he felt a compelling need to uncover its secrets. His journey began with the discovery of an old, tattered journal that hinted at a hidden truth, one that had been buried for centuries.

Little did Rajiv know that his quest would awaken the malevolent forces within Kaal Bhavan, setting off a chain of events that would test his courage, loyalty, and sanity. Joined by Ananya and Professor Mehta, Rajiv embarked on a perilous journey into the heart of darkness, where the line between reality and nightmare blurred, and the true nature of the curse was revealed.

As the shadows of Kaal Bhavan closed in around them, they would have to confront their deepest fears, make unthinkable sacrifices, and unravel the enigma of the relic. For in the end, only by facing the darkness within and without could they hope to break the curse and bring light to the haunted halls of Kaal Bhavan.

CHAPTER ONE

WHISPERS OF THE PAST

THE RELIC OF KAAL BHAVAN

The sun was setting over the ancient city of Varanasi, casting long shadows over the sacred ghats. The air was thick with the scent of incense and the sound of temple bells, blending seamlessly with the distant chants of priests performing evening rituals. The city, known as the spiritual heart of India, was a place where the line between the mortal and the divine seemed to blur. Here, time felt like an illusion, with past and present coexisting in a delicate balance. Rajiv Sharma stepped off the train at Varanasi Junction, feeling a chill despite the warm evening air.

At 35, Rajiv was a seasoned archaeologist with a reputation for solving some of the most intricate historical puzzles. His tall, lean frame and unkempt hair gave him an air of rugged determination, while his keen eyes missed nothing. Yet, this quest was personal.

His father, also an archaeologist, had disappeared mysteriously while searching for a relic believed to be connected to Lord Shiva. As Rajiv navigated through the bustling streets of Varanasi, he couldn't help but feel a sense of foreboding. The city was alive with activity—pilgrims performing rituals along the Ganges, vendors selling garlands of marigolds, and the ceaseless flow of people moving like a river through the narrow alleyways. The colorful chaos of Varanasi was overwhelming, a sensory overload that made Rajiv's task seem even more daunting. Street vendors called out to him, trying to sell him everything from spicy snacks to spiritual trinkets. Holy men, their bodies smeared with ash, sat in deep meditation, seemingly oblivious to the world around them. Tourists, wide-eyed and camera-laden, navigated the labyrinthine streets with a mixture of awe and trepidation. But beneath the vibrant surface, there was an undercurrent of something darker, something that seemed to whisper warnings to those who would listen. Rajiv's father had been obsessed with the legend of Kaal Bhavan, a mansion said to house an ancient and powerful relic. Locals whispered that the mansion was cursed, its walls haunted by the spirits of those who had dared to seek the relic. Despite the warnings, Rajiv felt compelled to continue his father's work and uncover the truth behind the mansion and its mysterious artifact. He made his way through the labyrinthine streets of Varanasi, guided by the directions in his father's journal.

The journal, worn and weathered, was a testament to years of research and exploration. Its pages were filled with sketches, notes, and cryptic symbols, all pointing to the elusive Kaal Bhavan. The detailed maps and annotations in the journal suggested that his father had come tantalizingly close to finding the relic.

The thought gave Rajiv a renewed sense of purpose, mingled with a pang of grief. He could almost feel his father's presence, urging him to press on. As he approached the outskirts of the city, the crowds thinned, and the air grew colder. The sun had dipped below the horizon, and the sky was painted with hues of purple and orange, giving way to the encroaching darkness. The mansions here were relics of a bygone era, their grandeur now faded into shadows of decay. The mansion loomed ahead, shrouded in an unnatural shadow that seemed to swallow the fading light of day.

Kaal Bhavan was a decaying structure, its once-grand facade now overrun with ivy and neglect. The mansion stood on a slight rise, its silhouette stark against the darkening sky. The windows were broken, their jagged edges like the teeth of some ancient beast, and the front door hung ajar, creaking ominously in the wind. The path leading to the mansion was overgrown with weeds, and the air was thick with the smell of damp earth and decay. Rajiv took a deep breath and stepped inside, the wooden floorboards groaning under his weight. The interior of the mansion was even more foreboding. Dust motes danced in the dim light that filtered through the broken windows, and the air was thick with the scent of mildew and rot. The walls were lined with peeling wallpaper, and cobwebs draped the corners like tattered veils. The silence was almost palpable, broken only by the distant sound of dripping water and the occasional scurrying of unseen creatures. He moved cautiously, his senses alert for any sign of danger or discovery. His footsteps echoed eerily through the empty halls as he made his way deeper into the mansion, guided by the entries in his father's journal.

Each step felt like a descent into the past, a journey through layers of forgotten history and hidden truths. The mansion seemed to breathe around him, the creaking of its wooden beams and the rustling of unseen creatures creating a symphony of unsettling sounds. Rajiv's flashlight flickered, casting dancing shadows on the walls that seemed to take on a life of their own. He paused at an old portrait, its once-vibrant colors faded with time. The eyes of the figure in the painting seemed to follow him, their gaze piercing and accusatory. The figure in the painting was that of a regal-looking man in traditional Indian attire, his expression stern and commanding.

The inscription at the bottom read: "Raja Indraveer Singh, 1865." Rajiv felt a shiver run down his spine as he stared into the painted eyes that seemed almost alive.

His father's notes had mentioned Raja Indraveer Singh as the original owner of Kaal Bhavan, a man rumored to have dabbled in dark rituals and forbidden knowledge. Rajiv's father had speculated that the Raja's obsession with the relic had driven him to madness, and perhaps even to his death. The whispers grew louder as Rajiv continued down the hallway. They seemed to be calling his name, the voices overlapping in a dissonant chorus. He turned a corner and found himself facing a large, ornately carved door. The wood was dark and polished, in stark contrast to the decaying surroundings. The handle was a bronze serpent, its eyes made of tiny rubies that glinted in the dim light. Rajiv hesitated, his hand hovering over the handle. The air was thick with tension, and he could feel his heart pounding in his chest. Taking a deep breath, he grasped the serpent handle and pushed the door open. The room beyond was a library, but unlike any library Rajiv had ever seen. The air was thick with dust, and the shelves were crammed with books of all shapes and sizes, their spines cracked and pages yellowed with age. The room was vast, its high ceilings lost in shadow, and the walls were lined with towering bookcases. At the center of the room stood a large, ornate desk, its surface cluttered with quills, ink bottles, and parchment. Rajiv approached the desk, his eyes drawn to a leather-bound journal lying open on its surface. He recognized the handwriting immediately—it was his father's journal. The pages were filled with detailed notes and sketches, all pertaining to the relic and its supposed location within the mansion. Rajiv's fingers trembled as he turned the pages, absorbing the information. His father's meticulous notes described secret passages, hidden chambers, and clues embedded in the very architecture of Kaal Bhavan. The whispers in the room grew louder, more insistent. They seemed to be coming from all around him, a chorus of ghostly voices speaking in a language he couldn't understand.

The sound was both haunting and mesmerizing, drawing him further into the depths of the mansion. Suddenly, the temperature in the room plummeted, and a figure emerged from the darkness. It was a ghostly apparition, its features twisted and grotesque. The spirit's eyes glowed with an unnatural light as it reached out toward Rajiv, its fingers curling like talons. Rajiv stumbled backward, his breath coming in short, panicked gasps. He could feel the cold seeping into his bones, sapping his strength. Desperation fueled his movements as he grabbed his father's journal and fled the room, the spirit's wails echoing behind him. He ran through the darkened halls, the mansion seeming to close in around him. The whispers had returned, louder and more frenzied, as if the very walls were alive with restless spirits. Rajiv burst through the front door, gasping for air as he stumbled into the night. As he looked back at the mansion, its windows glowed with an eerie light, and the whispers faded into the distance. Rajiv knew that he had only just begun to uncover the dark secrets of Kaal Bhavan. His father's journal held the key to the relic's location, but it was clear that the path ahead would be fraught with danger and terror. Determined to honor his father's legacy and solve the mystery of the relic, Rajiv steeled himself for the journey ahead. The shadows of Kaal Bhavan loomed large, but he was resolved to face whatever horrors lay within its walls.

Rajiv took a moment to catch his breath, clutching his father's journal tightly to his chest. The night air was cool and refreshing, a stark contrast to the oppressive atmosphere inside the mansion. He looked around, trying to get his bearings. The mansion stood isolated, surrounded by overgrown vegetation and ancient trees that seemed to whisper secrets of their own. He realized he needed a plan. The journal mentioned several key locations within the mansion that might hold clues to the relic's whereabouts. There was the basement, rumored to house a labyrinthine network of tunnels; the attic, where strange noises had been heard; and the courtyard, where an ancient well stood as a silent sentinel. Each location posed its own set of challenges and dangers, but Rajiv knew he had no choice but to explore them all. As he prepared to re-enter the mansion, he noticed a faint light flickering in one of the upper windows.

It was a The sun was setting over the ancient city of Varanasi, casting long shadows over the sacred ghats. The air was thick with the scent of incense and the sound of temple bells, blending seamlessly with the distant chants of priests performing evening rituals. The city, known as the spiritual heart of India, was a place where the line between the mortal and the divine seemed to blur. Here, time felt like an illusion, with past and present coexisting in a delicate balance. Rajiv Sharma stepped off the train at Varanasi Junction, feeling a chill despite the warm evening air. At 35, Rajiv was a seasoned archaeologist with a reputation for solving some of the most intricate historical puzzles.

His tall, lean frame and unkempt hair gave him an air of rugged determination, while his keen eyes missed nothing. Yet, this quest was personal. His father, also an archaeologist, had disappeared mysteriously while searching for a relic believed to be connected to Lord Shiva. As Rajiv navigated through the bustling streets of Varanasi, he couldn't help but feel a sense of foreboding. The city was alive with activity—pilgrims performing rituals along the Ganges, vendors selling garlands of marigolds, and the ceaseless flow of people moving like a river through the narrow alleyways.

The colorful chaos of Varanasi was overwhelming, a sensory overload that made Rajiv's task seem even more daunting. Street vendors called out to him, trying to sell him everything from spicy snacks to spiritual trinkets. Holy men, their bodies smeared with ash, sat in deep meditation, seemingly oblivious to the world around them. Tourists, wide-eyed and camera-laden, navigated the labyrinthine streets with a mixture of awe and trepidation. But beneath the vibrant surface, there was an undercurrent of something darker, something that seemed to whisper warnings to those who would listen. Rajiv's father had been obsessed with the legend of Kaal Bhavan, a mansion said to house an ancient and powerful relic.

Locals whispered that the mansion was cursed, its walls haunted by the spirits of those who had dared to seek the relic. Despite the warnings, Rajiv felt compelled to continue his father's work and uncover the truth behind the mansion and its mysterious artifact.

He made his way through the labyrinthine streets of Varanasi, guided by the directions in his father's journal. The journal, worn and weathered, was a testament to years of research and exploration. Its pages were filled with sketches, notes, and cryptic symbols, all pointing to the elusive Kaal Bhavan. The detailed maps and annotations in the journal suggested that his father had come tantalizingly close to finding the relic. The thought gave Rajiv a renewed sense of purpose, mingled with a pang of grief. He could almost feel his father's presence, urging him to press on.

As he approached the outskirts of the city, the crowds thinned, and the air grew colder. The sun had dipped below the horizon, and the sky was painted with hues of purple and orange, giving way to the encroaching darkness. The mansions here were relics of a bygone era, their grandeur now faded into shadows of decay. The mansion loomed ahead, shrouded in an unnatural shadow that seemed to swallow the fading light of day. Kaal Bhavan was a decaying structure, its once-grand facade now overrun with ivy and neglect. The mansion stood on a slight rise, its silhouette stark against the darkening sky.

The windows were broken, their jagged edges like the teeth of some ancient beast, and the front door hung ajar, creaking ominously in the wind. The path leading to the mansion was overgrown with weeds, and the air was thick with the smell of damp earth and decay. Rajiv took a deep breath and stepped inside, the wooden floorboards groaning under his weight. The interior of the mansion was even more foreboding. Dust motes danced in the dim light that filtered through the broken windows, and the air was thick with the scent of mildew and rot. The walls were lined with peeling wallpaper, and cobwebs draped the corners like tattered veils. The silence was almost palpable, broken only by the distant sound of dripping water and the occasional scurrying of unseen creatures. He moved cautiously, his senses alert for any sign of danger or discovery.

His footsteps echoed eerily through the empty halls as he made his way deeper into the mansion, guided by the entries in his father's journal.

Each step felt like a descent into the past, a journey through layers of forgotten history and hidden truths. The mansion seemed to breathe around him, the creaking of its wooden beams and the rustling of unseen creatures creating a symphony of unsettling sounds.

Rajiv's flashlight flickered, casting dancing shadows on the walls that seemed to take on a life of their own. He paused at an old portrait, its once-vibrant colors faded with time. The eyes of the figure in the painting seemed to follow him, their gaze piercing and accusatory. The figure in the painting was that of a regal-looking man in traditional Indian attire, his expression stern and commanding. The inscription at the bottom read: "Raja Indraveer Singh, 1865." Rajiv felt a shiver run down his spine as he stared into the painted eyes that seemed almost alive. His father's notes had mentioned Raja Indraveer Singh as the original owner of Kaal Bhavan, a man rumored to have dabbled in dark rituals and forbidden knowledge. Rajiv's father had speculated that the Raja's obsession with the relic had driven him to madness, and perhaps even to his death. The whispers grew louder as Rajiv continued down the hallway. They seemed to be calling his name, the voices overlapping in a dissonant chorus. He turned a corner and found himself facing a large, ornately carved door. The wood was dark and polished, in stark contrast to the decaying surroundings. The handle was a bronze serpent, its eyes made of tiny rubies that glinted in the dim light. Rajiv hesitated, his hand hovering over the handle.

The air was thick with tension, and he could feel his heart pounding in his chest.

Taking a deep breath, he grasped the serpent handle and pushed the door open. The room beyond was a library, but unlike any library Rajiv had ever seen. The air was thick with dust, and the shelves were crammed with books of all shapes and sizes, their spines cracked and pages yellowed with age. The room was vast, its high ceilings lost in shadow, and the walls were lined with towering bookcases. At the center of the room stood a large, ornate desk, its surface cluttered with quills, ink bottles, and parchment. Rajiv approached the desk, his eyes drawn to a leather-bound journal lying open on its surface. He recognized the handwriting immediately—it was his father's journal. The pages were filled with detailed notes and sketches, all pertaining to the relic and its supposed location within the mansion. Rajiv's fingers trembled as he turned the pages, absorbing the information. His father's meticulous notes described secret passages, hidden chambers, and clues embedded in the very architecture of Kaal Bhavan.

The whispers in the room grew louder, more insistent. They seemed to be coming from all around him, a chorus of ghostly voices speaking in a language he couldn't understand. The sound was both haunting and mesmerizing, drawing him further into the depths of the mansion. Suddenly, the temperature in the room plummeted, and a figure emerged from the darkness. It was a ghostly apparition, its features twisted and grotesque. The spirit's eyes glowed with an unnatural light as it reached out toward Rajiv, its fingers curling like talons. Rajiv stumbled backward, his breath coming in short, panicked gasps. He could feel the cold seeping into his bones, sapping his strength. Desperation fueled his movements as he grabbed his father's journal and fled the room, the spirit's wails echoing behind him.

He ran through the darkened halls, the mansion seeming to close in around him. The whispers had returned, louder and more frenzied, as if the very walls were alive with restless spirits. Rajiv burst through the front door, gasping for air as he stumbled into the night. As he looked back at the mansion, its windows glowed with an eerie light, and the whispers faded into the distance. Rajiv knew that he had only just begun to uncover the dark secrets of Kaal Bhavan. His father's journal held the key to the relic's location, but it was clear that the path ahead would be fraught with danger and terror. Determined to honor his father's legacy and solve the mystery of the relic, Rajiv steeled himself for the journey ahead. The shadows of Kaal Bhavan loomed large, but he was resolved to face whatever horrors lay within its walls. Rajiv took a moment to catch his breath, clutching his father's journal tightly to his chest. The night air was cool and refreshing, a stark contrast to the oppressive atmosphere inside the mansion. He looked around, trying to get his bearings. The mansion stood isolated, surrounded by overgrown vegetation and ancient trees that seemed to whisper secrets of their own.

He realized he needed a plan. The journal mentioned several key locations within the mansion that might hold clues to the relic's whereabouts. There was the basement, rumored to house a labyrinthine network of tunnels; the attic, where strange noises had been heard; and the courtyard, where an ancient well stood as a silent sentinel. Each location posed its own set of challenges and dangers, but Rajiv knew he had no choice but to explore them all. As he prepared to re-enter the mansion, he noticed a faint light flickering in one of the upper windows. It was a

CHAPTER TWO

THE GUARDIAN'S WARNING

Rajiv's breath came in shallow gasps as he stood outside Kaal Bhavan, clutching his father's journal tightly. The mansion loomed behind him, its dark silhouette stark against the night sky. The chilling encounter with the apparition had left him shaken, but his resolve was only strengthened. He had to uncover the truth about the relic and his father's disappearance. Determined, he made his way back to the heart of Varanasi, the city's vibrant energy a stark contrast to the oppressive atmosphere of the mansion. He needed answers, and he knew just where to start.

His father's old friend and fellow archaeologist, Professor Arun Mehta, lived nearby. If anyone could shed light on the cryptic notes in the journal, it was him. The streets of Varanasi were quieter now, the shops closing and the pilgrims retreating to their lodgings. The air was cool, and the soft glow of streetlights cast long shadows on the ancient buildings. Rajiv's mind raced as he walked, replaying the events of the evening and the terrifying encounter with the ghostly figure. Professor Mehta's house was a modest bungalow nestled in a quiet neighborhood. The garden was well-tended, with fragrant jasmine and hibiscus flowers adding a touch of serenity to the surroundings. Rajiv knocked on the door, his heart pounding with anticipation. After a few moments, the door creaked open, and Professor Mehta appeared. He was an elderly man with a kind face, his white hair and beard giving him a distinguished air. His eyes, though aged, sparkled with intelligence and curiosity. "Rajiv, my boy," he greeted warmly, ushering him inside. "I wasn't expecting you. What brings you here at this hour?" Rajiv wasted no time in explaining. "Professor, I need your help. It's about my father and Kaal Bhavan." The mention of Kaal Bhavan made Professor Mehta's expression darken. He led Rajiv to the study, a cozy room lined with bookshelves and artifacts from various archaeological expeditions. They sat down, and Rajiv handed over his father's journal. Professor Mehta's eyes widened as he flipped through the pages. "Your father was always a brave man, but his obsession with Kaal Bhavan worried me. This mansion... it's more than just a historical site. It's a place steeped in dark legends and mysteries.

" Rajiv leaned forward, eager for any insight. "What do you know about the relic? And why is the mansion so feared?"

The professor SIGHED; his gaze distant as he recalled the past.

"Kaal Bhavan was built by Raja Indraveer Singh in the late 19th century.

He was a man of great wealth and power, but also of deep curiosity about the mystical and the unknown. He sought to harness the power of a relic believed to be a fragment of Lord Shiva's trident, known as the Trisula Shard. Legends say that this relic holds immense power, capable of altering destinies and revealing hidden truths." "But with great power comes great danger. The relic is said to be cursed, bringing ruin to those who seek it with impure intentions. Raja Indraveer's obsession with the relic led to his downfall. He performed dark rituals, hoping to unlock its secrets, but instead, he unleashed a malevolent force. The mansion became a place of death and despair, and it's said that the spirits of those who perished there still haunt its halls." Rajiv listened intently, the pieces of the puzzle slowly coming together. "My father believed he could find the relic and use its power for good. But he vanished without a trace." Professor Mehta nodded solemnly. "Your father was a brilliant man, but he underestimated the dangers. If you're determined to follow in his footsteps, you must be prepared for the risks. The spirits of Kaal Bhavan are not to be taken lightly." Rajiv's resolve hardened.

"I have to find out what happened to him, and I have to uncover the truth about the relic. Whatever it takes."

The professor placed a reassuring hand on Rajiv's shoulder. "I understand. But promise me you'll be careful. The mansion holds many secrets, and not all of them are meant to be uncovered." Rajiv nodded, feeling a mix of fear and determination. He spent the next few hours with Professor Mehta, poring over the journal and discussing possible leads. The professor shared his own research, revealing maps and documents that hinted at hidden chambers and secret passages within Kaal Bhavan. As the night wore on, Rajiv felt a sense of clarity. He had a plan, and he had the knowledge he needed to continue his quest. But he also knew that he couldn't do it alone. The mansion's dark history and the malevolent forces within it required more than just courage; they required understanding and respect for the unknown. Before he left, Professor Mehta handed him a small, intricately carved wooden box. "Take this with you," he said.

"It's an old talisman, blessed by a revered sage. It may offer you some protection against the dark forces within Kaal Bhavan." Rajiv accepted the talisman gratefully, feeling its weight in his hand. It was a simple object, but it carried with it a sense of ancient power and hope. As he made his way back to his hotel, the streets of Varanasi were eerily quiet. The encounter with the apparition and the revelations from Professor Mehta weighed heavily on his mind. He knew that the path ahead would be fraught with danger, but he was determined to see it through. Back in his hotel room, Rajiv carefully studied the maps and notes, marking potential points of interest within the mansion. He formulated a plan, deciding to return to Kaal Bhavan at dawn, when the light would offer some comfort against the darkness. Sleep came fitfully, his dreams plagued by visions of the mansion and the ghostly figure that had attacked him. The whispers were there too, echoing in his mind, calling him back to Kaal Bhavan.

As the first light of dawn broke, Rajiv woke with a start. He gathered his belongings, including the talisman, and set out for the mansion once more. The journey through the awakening city was a stark contrast to the previous night. The streets were coming to life, with vendors setting up their stalls and pilgrims beginning their daily rituals. But Rajiv's focus was singular.

He had a mission, and nothing would deter him. As he approached Kaal Bhavan, the mansion seemed even more imposing in the early morning light. The shadows were less threatening, but the sense of foreboding remained. With renewed determination, Rajiv stepped through the gates of Kaal Bhavan. The journey into the mansion's depths would be perilous, but he was ready to face whatever lay ahead. The spirits of the past and the secrets of the relic awaited him, and he would not rest until he had uncovered the truth. Rajiv took a moment to catch his breath, clutching his father's journal tightly to his chest. The night air was cool and refreshing, a stark contrast to the oppressive atmosphere inside the mansion. He looked around, trying to get his bearings. The mansion stood isolated, surrounded by overgrown vegetation and ancient trees that seemed to whisper secrets of their own. He realized he needed a plan.

The journal mentioned several key locations within the mansion that might hold clues to the relic's whereabouts. There was the basement, rumored to house a labyrinthine network of tunnels; the attic, where strange noises had been heard; and the courtyard, where an ancient well stood as a silent sentinel. Each location posed its own set of challenges and dangers, but Rajiv knew he had no choice but to explore them all. As he prepared to re-enter the mansion, he noticed a faint light flickering in one of the upper windows. It was a small, unsteady glow, like that of a candle. Rajiv felt a shiver of apprehension but steeled himself and stepped through the front door once more. The interior was as foreboding as before, but this time Rajiv felt a strange sense of familiarity.

The house seemed almost to welcome him back, the creaking floors and whispering shadows guiding him forward. He moved carefully, following the maps and notes from his father's journal, making his way toward the basement first. The entrance to the basement was hidden behind a rotting tapestry. Rajiv pulled it aside, revealing a heavy wooden door with iron reinforcements. He took a deep breath and pushed it open. The air that greeted him was damp and musty, filled with the scent of earth and decay. He switched on his flashlight and descended the narrow staircase, each step echoing ominously in the confined space. The basement was a vast, labyrinthine expanse. Rajiv could see why his father had been so intrigued; the walls were lined with ancient symbols and intricate carvings. He moved slowly, examining each one, trying to decipher their meanings. His father's journal provided some guidance, but much of it was still shrouded in mystery. As he ventured deeper into the basement, Rajiv came across a series of alcoves, each containing relics and artifacts from different eras.

He paused to examine them, taking note of any that might relate to the Trishula Shard. One alcove held a small statue of Lord Shiva, its eyes seeming to follow him as he moved. Another contained a collection of scrolls, their brittle pages covered in strange, indecipherable script. Suddenly, Rajiv heard a faint sound, like a whisper carried on the wind. He turned, his flashlight beam cutting through the darkness.

At the far end of the basement, he saw a figure standing in the shadows. It was the same ghostly apparition he had encountered before, its eyes glowing with an eerie light. Rajiv felt a surge of fear but also a strange sense of.

CHAPTER THREE

THE HIDDEN CHAMBER

The morning sun had not yet fully banished the night as Rajiv stood before the imposing gates of Kaal Bhavan once more. The mansion seemed to loom even larger in the early light, its darkened WINDOWS-LIKE eyes watching his every move. He took a deep breath, gripping his father's journal tightly in one hand and the blessed talisman in the other. The eerie silence was occasionally broken by the distant calls of morning birds, a stark reminder of the world outside this haunted place. With determined steps, Rajiv pushed open the creaking gates and walked up the weed-choked path to the entrance. The front door yielded to his touch with a reluctant groan, and he stepped inside, immediately engulfed by the heavy, musty air. His footsteps echoed through the grand foyer, the dust motes dancing in the beam of his flashlight. This time, his purpose was clear. He headed straight for the library, where the haunting presence of the night before still lingered in his mind. The portraits lining the walls seemed to scrutinize him more intently, their painted eyes following his every move.

As he passed the portrait of Raja Indraveer Singh, he couldn't shake the feeling that the eyes were more than mere paint—there was an awareness in them that unnerved him.

In the library, Rajiv set the journal and talisman on the large mahogany desk. The leather-bound book lay open to the page that had led him here, its cryptic notes and sketches begging for further exploration. He carefully scanned the room, his flashlight revealing more details than he had noticed before. The bookshelves were filled with ancient texts, many of them written in Sanskrit and other long-forgotten languages. The smell of aged paper and leather was almost overwhelming. His father's notes had mentioned a specific carving that held a secret mechanism. Rajiv moved to the far wall where intricate carvings adorned the wooden paneling.

The scenes depicted were both beautiful and ominous, a stark contrast of divine serenity and chaotic battle. One carving in particular drew his attention—Lord Shiva wielding his trident, the Trishula, amidst a cosmic storm. The detail was exquisite, each line and contour painstakingly rendered. Rajiv ran his fingers over the carving, feeling for anything that might hint at a hidden latch. After several tense moments, his fingertips brushed against a small, almost imperceptible indentation. With a deep breath, he pressed it. The wall shuddered, and a narrow passageway slowly revealed itself, the mechanism creaking and groaning as if awakening from a long slumber. The air from the passageway was cooler and carried a faint metallic tang, mixed with the scent of damp earth. Rajiv hesitated only for a moment before stepping inside, the beam of his flashlight piercing the darkness ahead. The walls of the passage were rough stone, and the steps beneath his feet were worn and uneven, speaking of centuries of hidden use.

As he descended, the carvings continued along the walls, becoming more elaborate and otherworldly. They depicted scenes of ancient rituals, sacrifices, and the summoning of divine powers. The deeper he went, the more he felt an oppressive energy, as if the very stones around him were imbued with the echoes of past events. Finally, he reached the bottom of the stairs and emerged into a vast underground chamber. The sight took his breath away. The walls glowed faintly with an eerie blue light, casting long shadows that seemed to dance on their own. Ancient relics and artifacts filled the room, each one meticulously placed and exuding a palpable sense of history and power. At the center of the chamber stood a pedestal, and upon it rested a large, ornate chest. Rajiv approached it with reverence, his heart pounding in his chest. The chest was made of dark wood, inlaid with gold and precious stones, its surface covered in intricate patterns that mirrored the carvings above. It seemed to hum with an unseen energy, a relic of immense significance. He opened the chest with care, the hinges creaking in protest. Inside, resting on a bed of velvet, was the relic—an ancient shard of metal, glowing faintly with an inner light. The Trishula Shard. Rajiv's breath caught in his throat as he reached out to touch it. The shard was cool to the touch, its surface etched with arcane symbols that seemed to pulse with a life of their own. As his fingers brushed the relic, a surge of energy coursed through him. Visions flooded his mind—glimpses of the past, scenes of the rituals performed by Raja Indraveer Singh, and flashes of his father's face, his expression one of desperation and determination. The voices of the spirits echoed in his ears, a cacophony of whispers urging him to understand, to see the truth. The energy from the relic was overwhelming, and Rajiv staggered back, nearly dropping the shard. The chamber seemed to darken, the light dimming as an icy chill filled the air. He felt a presence behind him and turned to see the ghostly apparition from the previous night.

The spirit's eyes burned with an intense, malevolent light as it moved closer, its form shifting and flickering like a flame.

"You should not have come here,"

the spirit's voice was a low, guttural growl, filled with rage and sorrow. "The relic is not meant for mortals." Rajiv stood his ground, clutching the talisman tightly. "I need to know what happened to my father. Why did he disappear? What is the true nature of this relic?"

The spirit's form wavered, its expression torn between anger and something else—pain, perhaps, or regret. "Your father sought the relic with pure intentions, but he was deceived by its power. The curse claimed him, as it will claim you if you do not leave." Rajiv's mind raced. "But there must be a way to lift the curse, to use the relic's power for good. Isn't that why it was created?" The spirit's eyes softened momentarily. "There is a way, but it requires a great sacrifice. Only by offering something of immense value can the curse be broken." Before Rajiv could respond, the spirit vanished, leaving him alone in the chamber. The weight of its words hung heavily in the air. A great sacrifice. What could he possibly offer that would be enough to break the curse? Determined to find answers, Rajiv carefully placed the relic back in the chest and closed it. He needed to understand more about the curse and the sacrifice required. With a final glance around the chamber, he made his way back up the passageway, the echoes of the past still reverberating in his mind. As he emerged into the daylight, Rajiv felt a renewed sense of purpose.

The mansion's secrets were slowly unraveling, but there was still much to discover. The relic's power was real, and so was the curse that guarded it. He would need to dig deeper into the history of Kaal Bhavan and its dark legacy. Rajiv knew he couldn't do it alone. He needed allies, people who understood the mystical and the ancient. Professor Mehta was a start, but there were others—scholars, mystics, and perhaps even those who had survived encounters with the mansion's malevolent forces. With a plan forming in his mind, Rajiv set off to gather his allies.

The journey ahead would be perilous, but he was ready to face it. The whispers of the past were growing louder, and the truth about Kaal Bhavan and the relic lay just beyond the shadows.

CHAPTER FOUR

WHISPERS IN THE SHADOWS

The evening had turned into night by the time Rajiv returned to his hotel. His mind was racing with thoughts of the relic and the spirit's warning. The bustling streets of Varanasi, usually so full of life, felt eerie under the dim glow of streetlights. Shadows stretched long and dark across the ancient buildings, and the familiar sounds of the city seemed muted, as if even the city itself held its breath, aware of the dark secrets Rajiv was unearthing.

Sleep was elusive. Each time Rajiv closed his eyes, visions of Kaal Bhavan and the ghostly apparition haunted him. His father's face appeared repeatedly in his dreams, contorted with fear and desperation. The whispers of the spirits grew louder in his mind, their unintelligible words filling him with dread and a sense of urgency. When exhaustion finally overtook him, it was a restless sleep filled with fragmented, unsettling dreams. At the break of dawn, Rajiv awoke with a start, his heart pounding. The morning light seeped through the thin curtains of his hotel room, casting long, slanted shadows on the walls. He felt an urgent need to return to Kaal Bhavan, compelled by an unexplainable force. After a quick breakfast, he packed his bag with essential supplies,

including the talisman and his father's journal, and set off once more for the mansion. The journey through the awakening city was a blur. Rajiv's thoughts were consumed by the mystery of the relic and the spirit's cryptic message about a great sacrifice. What could be valuable enough to lift the curse? His father's face haunted him, urging him to find the answers he sought. As Rajiv approached Kaal Bhavan, the mansion stood in stark contrast to the vibrant city around it.

The decaying structure seemed to suck the light from the sky, casting an ominous shadow over the surrounding area. The air grew colder as he neared the gates, a chill that seeped into his bones. He hesitated at the threshold, the memory of his last encounter with the spirit fresh in his mind. But the pull of the mystery was too strong to resist. He stepped through the gates and made his way to the entrance, the heavy door groaning in protest as he pushed it open. Inside, the air was thick with dust and the smell of decay, the oppressive silence only broken by the occasional creak of the old mansion settling. Rajiv's flashlight cut through the darkness, illuminating the grand foyer with its faded grandeur and cobweb-covered chandeliers. This time, he headed for the east wing of the mansion, guided by a hunch and the vague hints in his father's notes.

The east wing had been off-limits during his previous explorations, but now he felt a compulsion to uncover its secrets. As he walked through the darkened corridors, he couldn't shake the feeling of being watched. The eyes of the portraits seemed to follow him, and every shadow seemed to conceal a hidden threat. The atmosphere grew more oppressive as he ventured deeper into the mansion. The air became thicker, almost suffocating, and the temperature dropped noticeably. Rajiv's breath formed visible puffs in the cold, and he pulled his jacket tighter around himself. The floorboards creaked under his weight, the sound echoing ominously in the silent halls. He came upon a door at the end of the corridor, its surface adorned with strange, arcane symbols that seemed to pulse with an eerie light. Rajiv hesitated, feeling a sense of foreboding, but his curiosity and determination pushed him forward.

He reached out and touched the door, feeling a surge of cold energy pass through him. The door swung open with a reluctant creak, revealing a dark, narrow staircase descending into the depths of the mansion. The stairs were steep and treacherous, each step echoing like a drumbeat in the confined space. The walls were lined with more of the strange symbols, their glow providing the only light in the darkness. As he descended, Rajiv could feel the air grow colder and heavier, filled with a palpable sense of dread. The whispers of the spirits grew louder, their voices overlapping in a dissonant chorus that set his nerves on edge. At the bottom of the stairs,

Rajiv found himself in another underground chamber, larger and more elaborate than the one he had discovered before. The walls were covered in detailed murals depicting scenes of sacrifice and dark rituals, their vivid imagery almost too realistic.

The room was filled with ancient relics and artifacts, each one exuding a sense of malevolent power. In the center of the chamber stood a large stone altar, its surface stained with what appeared to be dried blood. The sight sent a chill down Rajiv's spine, and he could feel the oppressive energy of the place pressing down on him. As he approached the altar, the whispers grew louder, more insistent, filling his mind with fragmented images and cryptic messages. Rajiv reached out and touched the altar, feeling a surge of cold energy pass through him. Visions flooded his mind—scenes of dark rituals performed by hooded figures, sacrifices made in the name of power, and the anguished faces of those who had perished in the mansion. Among the visions, he saw his father, bound and desperate, struggling against unseen forces. The sight filled him with a sense of urgency and determination. As the visions faded, Rajiv noticed a hidden compartment at the base of the altar. He knelt down and carefully opened it, revealing a small, ornate box. The box was made of dark wood, inlaid with gold and precious stones, and its surface was covered in the same arcane symbols that adorned the walls.

With trembling hands, Rajiv opened the box, revealing a piece of parchment and a small vial of dark liquid. The parchment was covered in ancient script, its meaning unclear. But as Rajiv studied it, he felt a strange connection to the words, as if they were speaking directly to him. The vial of liquid seemed to pulse with an inner light, its contents swirling with an unnatural energy. Before he could make sense of the discovery, a cold wind swept through the chamber, extinguishing his flashlight. Rajiv was plunged into darkness, the oppressive energy of the room closing in around him. He felt a presence behind him and turned to see the ghostly apparition from before, its eyes burning with an intense, malevolent light. "You should not have come here," the spirit's voice was a low, guttural growl, filled with rage and sorrow.

"The relic is not meant for mortals."

Rajiv stood his ground, clutching the talisman tightly. "I need to know what happened to my father. Why did he disappear? What is the true nature of this relic?" The spirit's form wavered, its expression torn between anger and something else—pain, perhaps, or regret. "Your father sought the relic with pure intentions, but he was deceived by its power. The curse claimed him, as it will claim you if you do not leave." Rajiv's mind raced. "But there must be a way to lift the curse, to use the relic's power for good. Isn't that why it was created?" The spirit's eyes softened momentarily. "There is a way, but it requires a great sacrifice. Only by offering something of immense value can the curse be broken." Before Rajiv could respond, the spirit vanished, leaving him alone in the chamber.

The weight of its words hung heavily in the air.

A great sacrifice. What could he possibly offer that would be enough to break the curse? Determined to find answers, Rajiv carefully placed the relic back in the chest and closed it. He needed to understand more about the curse and the sacrifice required. With a final glance around the chamber, he made his way back up the passageway, the echoes of the past still reverberating in his mind. As he emerged into the daylight, Rajiv felt a renewed sense of purpose. The mansion's secrets were slowly unraveling, but there was still much to discover. The relic's power was real, and so was the curse that guarded it. He would need to dig deeper into the history of Kaal Bhavan and its dark legacy. Rajiv knew he couldn't do it alone.

He needed allies, people who understood the mystical and the ancient. Professor Mehta was a start, but there were others—scholars, mystics, and perhaps even those who had survived encounters with the mansion's malevolent forces.

With a plan forming in his mind, Rajiv set off to gather his allies. The journey ahead would be perilous, but he was ready to face it. The whispers of the past were growing louder, and the truth about Kaal Bhavan and the relic lay just beyond the shadows.

CHAPTER FIVE

ECHOES OF THE PAST

Rajiv felt an almost physical pull as he left Kaal Bhavan and walked back to his hotel. The morning sun was high in the sky, casting long, eerie shadows across the city streets. Despite the heat, a chill clung to his bones, the lingering presence of the mansion's oppressive energy following him like a specter. At the hotel, Rajiv wasted no time in reaching out to Professor Mehta. He had barely slept, and the exhaustion was evident in his voice as he explained his latest discoveries. The professor listened INTENTLY; his silence punctuated by the occasional thoughtful hum. "You've done well to find the altar and the relic," Mehta said finally. "But this is only the beginning. The script you described on the parchment, it sounds like an ancient form of Sanskrit, used in specific rituals. I will need to see it to decipher its full meaning."

Rajiv agreed to meet the professor at the university that afternoon. As he packed the relic and his father's journal, he felt the weight of the spirits' whispers pressing against his mind, urging him forward but also warning him of the dangers ahead. The university campus was bustling with activity when Rajiv arrived. Students and professors moved between buildings, engrossed in their own worlds, oblivious to the dark secrets Rajiv carried with him. Professor Mehta met him in his cluttered office, its walls lined with books and artifacts from various ancient cultures. Rajiv carefully placed the relic and the parchment on the professor's desk. Mehta examined them with a mix of awe and trepidation, his fingers tracing the intricate designs on the box and the parchment. "This script is incredibly old," Mehta murmured. "It speaks of a powerful relic, created to harness the energies of the universe. But it also warns of the curse that binds it, a curse that can only be broken by a great sacrifice." "What kind of sacrifice?" Rajiv asked, his voice barely above a whisper.

The professor looked up, his eyes grave. "It's not clear, but the sacrifice must be something of immense personal value. Not just any offering will do. It must be something that holds significant meaning to the person seeking to break the curse."

Rajiv felt a cold dread settle in his stomach. The implications were clear—he would have to give up something deeply precious to him. But what? And would it be enough? As they continued to discuss the relic, a sudden knock on the door interrupted them. A young woman entered, her eyes wide with excitement. She introduced herself as Ananya, a graduate student specializing in ancient texts and rituals. "Professor, I couldn't help but overhear,

" she said, glancing at Rajiv. "I've been studying similar rituals in ancient texts.

There's a reference to a hidden chamber within Kaal Bhavan that might hold more answers." Rajiv felt a spark of hope. "Do you know where this chamber is?" Ananya nodded. "The texts are vague, but they mention a hidden passage beneath the mansion, accessible only during a specific lunar phase. Coincidentally, tonight is one of those phases." The professor looked at Rajiv.

"It seems the mansion is revealing more secrets. You should investigate this chamber. Ananya and I will continue to study the relic and the parchment." That night, Rajiv returned to Kaal Bhavan with renewed determination. The mansion loomed in the darkness, its windows like empty, watching eyes. He felt a shiver run down his spine as he crossed the threshold, the air inside even colder and heavier than before. Following Ananya's directions, Rajiv made his way to the mansion's basement. The stone walls were damp and covered in moss, the air thick with the smell of decay.

He found the spot she had described—a section of the wall marked with faint, ancient symbols. Using his flashlight, Rajiv examined the wall closely. His heart raced as he noticed a small indentation shaped like the relic's symbols. With trembling hands, he pressed the talisman against the indentation. The wall groaned and shifted, revealing a narrow passage descending into the darkness. Rajiv stepped into the passage, the air growing colder with each step. The whispers of the spirits grew louder, more insistent, filling his mind with fragmented images and cryptic messages. He felt a presence watching him, the weight of the mansion's dark history pressing down on him. The passage opened into a hidden chamber, larger and more elaborate than the others he had seen.

The walls were covered in intricate carvings depicting scenes of sacrifice and dark rituals, their vivid imagery almost too realistic. The air was thick with a palpable sense of dread, and Rajiv could feel the oppressive energy of the place pressing down on him. In the center of the chamber stood a large stone altar, its surface stained with what appeared to be dried blood. The sight sent a chill down Rajiv's spine, and he could feel the oppressive energy of the place pressing down on him. As he approached the altar, the whispers grew louder, more insistent, filling his mind with fragmented images and cryptic messages.

Rajiv reached out and touched the altar, feeling a surge of cold energy pass through him. Visions flooded his mind—scenes of dark rituals performed by hooded figures, sacrifices made in the name of power, and the anguished faces of those who had perished in the mansion. Among the visions, he saw his father, bound and desperate, struggling against unseen forces. The sight filled him with a sense of urgency and determination. As the visions faded, Rajiv noticed a hidden compartment at the base of the altar. He knelt down and carefully opened it, revealing a small, ornate box.

The box was made of dark wood, inlaid with gold and precious stones, and its surface was covered in the same arcane symbols that adorned the walls. With trembling hands, Rajiv opened the box, revealing a piece of parchment and a small vial of dark liquid. The parchment was covered in ancient script, its meaning unclear. But as Rajiv studied it, he felt a strange connection to the words, as if they were speaking directly to him. The vial of liquid seemed to pulse with an inner light, its contents swirling with an unnatural energy. Before he could make sense of the discovery, a cold wind swept through the chamber, extinguishing his flashlight. Rajiv was plunged into darkness, the oppressive energy of the room closing in around him. He felt a presence behind him and turned to see the ghostly apparition from before, its eyes burning with an intense, malevolent light.

"You should not have come here," the spirit's voice was a low, guttural growl, filled with rage and sorrow.

"The relic is not meant for mortals." Rajiv stood his ground, clutching the talisman tightly. "I need to know what happened to my father. Why did he disappear? What is the true nature of this relic?" The spirit's form wavered, its expression torn between anger and something else—pain, perhaps, or regret. "Your father sought the relic with pure intentions, but he was deceived by its power. The curse claimed him, as it will claim you if you do not leave." Rajiv's mind raced. "But there must be a way to lift the curse, to use the relic's power for good. Isn't that why it was created?" The spirit's eyes softened momentarily. "There is a way, but it requires a great sacrifice. Only by offering something of immense value can the curse be broken." Before Rajiv could respond, the spirit vanished, leaving him alone in the chamber. The weight of its words hung heavily in the air. A great sacrifice. What could he possibly offer that would be enough to break the curse? Determined to find answers, Rajiv carefully placed the relic back in the chest and closed it. He needed to understand more about the curse and the sacrifice required. With a final glance around the chamber, he made his way back up the passageway, the echoes of the past still reverberating in his mind. As he emerged into the daylight, Rajiv felt a renewed sense of purpose. The mansion's secrets were slowly unraveling, but there was still much to discover. The relic's power was real, and so was the curse that guarded it. He would need to dig deeper into the history of Kaal Bhavan and its dark legacy. Rajiv knew he couldn't do it alone. He needed allies, people who understood the mystical and the ancient. Professor Mehta was a start, but there were others—scholars, mystics, and perhaps even those who had survived encounters with the mansion's malevolent forces. With a plan forming in his mind, Rajiv set off to gather his allies. The journey ahead would be perilous, but he was ready to face it.

The whispers of the past were growing louder, and the truth about Kaal Bhavan and the relic lay just beyond the shadows.

As Rajiv walked back through the city, his thoughts were interrupted by an uneasy feeling that gnawed at him. He had the distinct impression that he was being followed. Glancing over his shoulder, he saw nothing out of the ordinary, but the feeling persisted. When he reached his hotel, he quickly scanned the lobby, noticing a figure sitting in the corner, half-hidden in shadows.

The man appeared to be reading a newspaper, but Rajiv could feel his eyes on him. With his heart pounding, Rajiv made his way to the elevators, his senses on high alert. Once inside his room, he locked the door and drew the curtains, creating a barrier between himself and the outside world. He knew he couldn't afford to be paranoid, but the mansion's influence was pervasive.

He needed to stay focused and gather his allies. That evening, Rajiv met with Professor Mehta and Ananya at a secluded café. The atmosphere was tense as they discussed

CHAPTER SIX

SHADOWS IN THE NIGHT

Rajiv, Professor Mehta, and Ananya sat at a dimly lit table in the back corner of the café, the warm glow of the candles casting long, flickering shadows. The tension was palpable as they shared the discoveries made in Kaal Bhavan, their voices low and hushed.

Ananya spread out several old, leather-bound books across the table, each one brimming with ancient scripts and illustrations of dark rituals. "These texts mention various sacrifices, but they also speak of a guardian, a mysterious figure who is said to protect the secrets of the mansion."

Professor Mehta NODDED; his brow furrowed in concentration. "If this guardian exists, they could be the key to understanding the full extent of the curse and the sacrifice needed to lift it."

Rajiv felt a chill run down his spine. "How do we find this guardian?" Ananya leaned in, her voice barely above a whisper. "The texts are unclear, but there are mentions of a figure known as 'The Watcher.' They are said to appear to those who seek the truth, guiding them through the darkness. We need to summon them." Before they could discuss further, the door of the café swung open, and a cold breeze swept through the room. A tall, gaunt figure stepped INSIDE; his eyes hidden beneath the brim of a wide, dark hat. His presence seemed to suck the warmth out of the room, and a hush fell over the patrons as they turned to look at him.

Rajiv felt an inexplicable sense of dread as the man approached their table, his movements eerily fluid. He stopped just short of their table, his eyes scanning the books and artifacts spread out before them. "I hear you're seeking answers about Kaal Bhavan," the stranger said, his voice a low, gravelly whisper that seemed to resonate with the very bones of those who heard it.

Professor Mehta regarded the man cautiously. "Who are you?"

The stranger removed his hat, revealing sharp, angular features and piercing, ice-blue eyes that seemed to see through them. "I am known as Mr. D'Souza. I have studied the mansion and its dark history for many years. If you truly wish to uncover its secrets, I can help you." Rajiv exchanged a wary glance with the professor and Ananya. "What do you know about the guardian? The Watcher?" Mr. D'Souza's eyes narrowed. "The Watcher is a spectral guardian, bound to the mansion by a curse as old as time. They protect the relic and the dark secrets of Kaal Bhavan. Summoning them is no easy task, and it comes with great peril." Ananya leaned FORWARD; her curiosity piqued. "How do we summon the Watcher?" Mr. D'Souza pulled a small, leather-bound journal from his coat pocket and placed it on the table. "This contains the ritual you need.

But be warned—the Watcher is not benevolent. They test those who seek their knowledge, and failure to meet their demands can result in dire consequences." Rajiv picked up the journal, feeling the weight of its significance. "What kind of test?" The man's expression grew darker. "The Watcher will test your resolve, your courage, and your willingness to make sacrifices. Only those who prove worthy can gain the knowledge needed to break the curse." As Mr. D'Souza turned to leave, Rajiv called after him. "Why are you helping us?" The stranger paused, his gaze lingering on Rajiv. "Because I, too, have lost someone to the mansion's curse. Perhaps, together, we can end its reign of terror." With that, Mr. D'Souza disappeared into the night, leaving Rajiv and his companions with more questions than answers. They sat in silence for a moment, the weight of their task settling heavily upon them. "Let's go back to my office and examine this journal," Professor Mehta suggested, breaking the silence. They quickly gathered their belongings and made their way to the university. The campus was eerily quiet at night, the usually bustling hallways now empty and echoing with their footsteps. They settled into Mehta's office, the flickering lamplight casting unsettling shadows on the walls. Rajiv opened the journal, its pages yellowed with age and filled with dense, spidery handwriting. The ritual was detailed and complex, involving symbols, incantations, and specific times aligned with the lunar cycle. As they studied the ritual, the air in the room grew colder, and the shadows seemed to deepen. "We'll need to perform this ritual at Kaal Bhavan," Ananya said, her voice steady despite the growing unease. "It's the only way to summon the Watcher." Professor Mehta nodded. "We should prepare ourselves. The ritual requires absolute focus and determination. There can be no hesitation." The next night, the moon hung low and full in the sky, casting a pale, ghostly light over the city. Rajiv, Professor Mehta, and Ananya returned to Kaal BHAVAN their nerves taut with anticipation. They brought with them the necessary items for the ritual: candles, incense, and the journal detailing the incantations. As they entered the mansion, a sense of foreboding washed over them. The air was thick with the scent of decay, and the oppressive energy seemed even more palpable than before.

They made their way to the main hall, where they set up the ritual space, placing candles at the points of a pentagram drawn in chalk on the floor. The mansion seemed to come alive around them, the walls creaking and groaning as if in protest.

Rajiv felt a cold sweat break out on his forehead as he began the incantation, his voice echoing through the dark, empty halls. The candles flickered wildly, their flames dancing as if moved by an unseen force. As the ritual progressed, the temperature in the room dropped sharply, their breath visible in the cold air. The shadows around them grew darker, deeper, as if they were alive and moving. Rajiv's voice grew louder, more insistent, as he recited the final lines of the incantation. Suddenly, a deafening silence fell over the mansion, and the candles were snuffed out, plunging them into complete darkness. Rajiv felt a presence behind him, cold and malevolent. He turned slowly, his heart pounding in his chest. Before him stood a figure cloaked in shadow, its eyes glowing with an eerie, otherworldly light. The Watcher had arrived. "You have summoned me," the Watcher's voice was a low, chilling whisper that seemed to echo from the depths of the mansion itself. "Why do you seek the secrets of Kaal Bhavan?" Rajiv took a deep breath, steeling himself. "We seek to understand the relic and the curse that binds it. We want to break the curse and free those who have suffered because of it." The Watcher's eyes narrowed, and a cold, humorless smile crossed its face. "You seek to break the curse? Very well. But first, you must prove your worth." The air around them grew colder still, and the shadows seemed to close in, pressing against their minds. The Watcher raised a skeletal hand, and the room was filled with the sound of whispering voices, their words unintelligible but filled with a sense of dread.

"You must face your deepest fears,"

the Watcher intoned. "Only by confronting the darkness within can you hope to overcome the darkness without." As the Watcher spoke, Rajiv felt the world around him shift and change. He was no longer in the mansion, but in a dark, twisted version of his childhood home. The walls were covered in strange symbols, and the air was thick with the scent of blood and decay. He heard the sound of footsteps approaching, slow and deliberate. Rajiv turned to see his father standing before him, his eyes hollow and filled with despair. "Rajiv," his father's voice was a hoarse whisper, filled with pain. "Why did you leave me?" Rajiv's heart ached as he reached out to his father, but his hand passed through the apparition as if it were made of smoke. "I didn't leave you, Dad. I'm here to find you, to save you." His father's image flickered and distorted, his voice growing more desperate. "You can't save me.

The darkness has claimed me, and it will claim you too." Rajiv felt a surge of fear and guilt, the weight of his father's words pressing down on him. But he forced himself to stand firm, his resolve hardening. "No, I will not let the darkness win.

I will break the curse and free you." The apparition of his father let out a guttural scream, and the world around Rajiv shattered like glass, leaving him once again in the cold, dark mansion. He was gasping for breath, his heart racing, but he had faced his fear and emerged stronger for it. The Watcher's eyes glowed with a COLD malevolent light as it regarded Rajiv.

"You have passed the first test. But there is more to come." Next, the Watcher turned its gaze to Ananya, who was visibly trembling but determined to face whatever came next. The shadows around her swirled and coalesced, forming the image of a young girl, her eyes wide with terror. "Ananya," the girl's voice was a childlike whisper, filled with fear.

"Why did you let me die?"

Ananya's eyes filled with tears as she reached out to the girl. "I didn't want to, I tried to save you. I swear I did." The girl's form flickered, her expression one of sadness and accusation. "You failed. You let the darkness take me." Ananya's sobs echoed through the

THE PRICE OF KNOWLEDGE

The air inside Kaal Bhavan grew heavier, laden with an almost tangible darkness as the Watcher turned its gaze from Rajiv to Ananya. The shadows around them seemed to whisper secrets of the past, weaving a tapestry of fear and despair. Rajiv watched in horror as Ananya's sobs echoed through the mansion, her confrontation with the spectral girl revealing deep, unhealed wounds.

The Watcher's voice, cold and merciless, pierced the oppressive silence. "You must each face the darkness within you. Only then can you hope to uncover the secrets of Kaal Bhavan. Prepare yourselves, for the final test will demand a sacrifice." Ananya, tears streaming down her face, looked to Rajiv and Professor Mehta for strength. Her voice trembled as she spoke. "We have to do this. For everyone who has suffered because of this curse.

" Rajiv nodded, his resolve hardening. "We're in this together."

The Watcher raised its skeletal hand, and the room transformed. The walls of the mansion faded away, replaced by a vast, shadowy expanse. They stood in a desolate landscape, the ground covered in a thick layer of ash and the air filled with the acrid smell of burning flesh. A large stone altar stood in the center of the wasteland, stained with blood and surrounded by grotesque effigies of tormented souls. The Watcher floated above the altar, its eyes glowing with a malevolent light.

"The time has come for the sacrifice," it intoned. "One must give their life willingly, so the others may proceed." Rajiv's heart pounded in his chest. The air was thick with fear and tension. Ananya stepped forward, her face pale but determined. "If this is the only way to end the curse, I will do it." Professor Mehta grabbed her arm, his voice urgent.

"No, Ananya! There has to be another way."

The Watcher's gaze bore into them. "There is no other way.

The sacrifice must be made, and it must be given freely." Rajiv felt a wave of desperation wash over him. "We'll find another way. We have to." Suddenly, a chilling laughter echoed through the wasteland. Mr. D'Souza emerged from the SHADOWS; his eyes gleaming with madness. "You think you can cheat the curse?

It demands blood, and it will have it." Rajiv stared at him in shock. "You... you're part of this?" Mr. D'Souza's smile widened, revealing rows of sharp, yellowed teeth. "I've been watching you all along, guiding you to this moment. The curse of Kaal Bhavan is ancient, and it cannot be broken without a price." Before they could react, Mr. D'Souza lunged at Ananya, his hands reaching for her throat. Rajiv and Professor Mehta tried to intervene, but an invisible force held them back, paralyzing them with fear. Ananya struggled against Mr. D'Souza's GRIP her eyes wide with terror.

"Rajiv, help me!"

The Watcher observed impassively, its eyes glowing brighter as the struggle continued. Rajiv fought against the force holding him, his mind racing. He had to do something, anything to save Ananya. With a surge of adrenaline, Rajiv broke free of the invisible bonds and rushed at Mr. D'Souza, tackling him to the ground. They wrestled on the ashen ground, each fighting with a primal fury. Suddenly, a blinding light enveloped the altar, and the ground beneath them trembled. The Watcher's voice boomed, reverberating through the wasteland. "The sacrifice is made." Rajiv looked up in horror to see Ananya standing on the altar, a ceremonial dagger in her hand, her eyes filled with resignation. "I'm sorry, Rajiv. This is the only way." Before anyone could stop her, Ananya plunged the dagger into her chest. Blood poured from the wound, staining the altar red. Rajiv screamed, his voice raw with anguish. The Watcher's eyes flared with a blinding light, and the landscape around them began to dissolve. The shadows receded, and they were once again in the main hall of Kaal Bhavan. Ananya lay motionless on the floor, the dagger still embedded in her chest. Rajiv rushed to Her side, tear steaming down face "Ananya, no please wake up. Professor Mehta knelt beside him his own eyes wet with tears. "She sacrificed herself for us. For everyone." The Watcher hovered above them, its expression inscrutable.

"The sacrifice has been accepted.

You now possess the knowledge to end the curse." Rajiv looked up at the spectral figure, his voice trembling with rage and grief. "What do we do?" The Watcher raised its hand, and a glowing, ancient tome appeared before them. "Within these pages lies the ritual to destroy the relic and lift the curse. But beware-the path ahead is fraught with danger." Rajiv took the tome, his hands shaking. He looked at Ananya's lifeless body, his heart breaking. "We'll do whatever it takes." As they prepared to leave the mansion, the Watcher spoke one last time.

"Remember, the darkness is always watching. Should you fail, it will claim more lives." Rajiv, Professor Mehta, and the now deceased Ananya had paid a terrible price. But they were closer than ever to ending the nightmare that was Kaal Bhavan.

With heavy hearts and the ancient tome in hand, they stepped out of the mansion, the weight of their mission pressing down on them. The night was eerily silent as they made their way back to the university. The ritual to end the curse was within their grasp, but the cost had been immense.

As Rajiv and Professor Mehta began to decipher the tome's cryptic instructions, they couldn't shake the feeling that the darkness was still watching, waiting for another chance to claim their souls.

CHAPTER EIGHT

The Final Confrontation

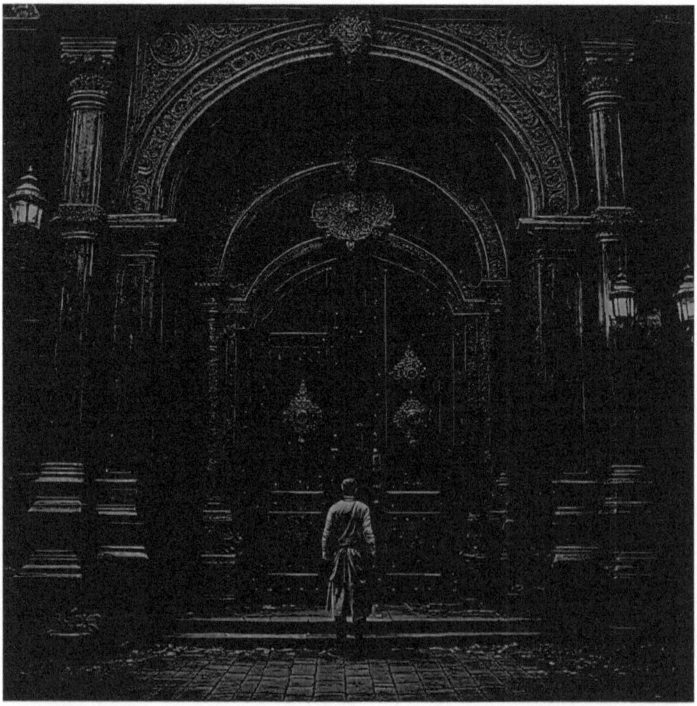

PART 2 :SHADOWS OF REDEMPTION

The ancient tome lay open on the table in Professor Mehta's office, its pages illuminated by the soft glow of candlelight. Rajiv and Professor Mehta studied the intricate diagrams and cryptic incantations, their minds racing with the weight of their mission. Ananya's sacrifice weighed heavily on them, a constant reminder of the perilous path they had chosen.

"The ritual seems straightforward enough," Professor Mehta muttered, tracing a finger over the ancient text. "But there are symbols here I've never seen before.

We must proceed with caution." Rajiv nodded, his thoughts still haunted by the memory of Ananya's lifeless body in Kaal Bhavan.

"We can't afford any mistakes. Lives depend on us." As they delved deeper into the ritual, the air in the room grew colder, and the candles flickered ominously. Shadows danced on the walls, twisting and contorting as if alive. Rajiv's skin prickled with unease, a sense of being watched settling over him like a suffocating blanket. Suddenly, a voice echoed through the room, low and guttural. "You dare to challenge the darkness?" Rajiv and Professor Mehta looked up to see Mr. D'Souza standing in the doorway, his eyes gleaming with madness. "You fool! The curse cannot be broken!" Rajiv's fists clenched with fury. "We've come too far to turn back now.

" Mr. D'Souza's laughter filled the room, grating and unhinged. "You think you can control the power within Kaal Bhavan? You're nothing but puppets in its grand design." Professor Mehta stood tall, his voice steady despite the rising tension. "Enough, D'Souza. We know the truth now, and we won't let you stop us." With a snarl, Mr. D'Souza lunged at them, his movements unnaturally swift.

Rajiv and Professor Mehta scrambled to defend themselves, but Mr. D'Souza seemed to possess a strength and agility beyond human capabilities. As they grappled with their adversary, the ancient tome slipped from the table and fell open to a page depicting a grotesque ritual circle. The symbols pulsed with an eerie light, and a chill wind swept through the room, carrying with it the faint scent of decay. In the midst of their struggle, a shadowy figure materialized in the center of the ritual circle.

The Watcher had returned, its eyes blazing with a cold, malevolent fury. "You dare to disrupt the balance," the Watcher's voice echoed through the room, commanding and implacable. "The time has come to end this." Mr. D'Souza froze, his eyes widening in terror as he beheld the spectral figure. "No... it can't be..." With a wave of its hand, the Watcher lifted Mr. D'Souza off the ground, suspending him in mid-air. Dark tendrils snaked around Mr. D'Souza's body, binding him tightly. "You have meddled in affairs beyond your understanding," the Watcher intoned. "For this, there must be consequences." Rajiv and Professor Mehta watched in stunned silence as the Watcher's form shimmered and expanded, growing larger and more imposing. Its eyes bore into Mr. D'Souza with an intensity that seemed to pierce his very soul. "Your punishment shall be eternal," the Watcher declared, its voice reverberating through the room. "May your spirit wander in torment for all eternity." With a final, agonized scream, Mr. D'Souza vanished into thin air, leaving behind only a lingering echo of his despair. Rajiv and Professor Mehta exchanged a glance, their hearts pounding with a mixture of relief and awe. The Watcher turned to them, its gaze softening ever so slightly. "You have faced the darkness and emerged victorious," the Watcher acknowledged. "But the true test lies ahead." With those cryptic words, the Watcher dissipated into a swirl of shadows, leaving Rajiv and Professor Mehta alone in the silent room. The candles burned low, their flickering light casting long, wavering shadows on the walls. "We have to perform the ritual," Rajiv said, his voice barely above a whisper. "We can't let Ananya's sacrifice be in vain.

" Professor Mehta nodded solemnly, his expression grave. "Prepare yourself, Rajiv. The fate of everyone trapped in the curse rests on this."

They gathered their resolve, steeling themselves for the final confrontation with the darkness that had plagued Kaal Bhavan for centuries. With trembling hands, they began the intricate incantations, their voices blending into a harmonious chant that echoed through the mansion. As they reached the crescendo of the ritual, the room seemed to tremble around them. Shadows coalesced into swirling vortexes, and the very air crackled with supernatural energy. The ancient symbols on the floor glowed with an intense, otherworldly light, casting their faces in stark relief. Just as they neared the culmination of the ritual, a deafening roar shook the mansion to its foundation. The ground beneath them trembled violently, sending waves of terror through their hearts. A monstrous figure materialized before them, its form twisted and contorted, a grotesque amalgamation of nightmares. Rajiv's breath caught in his throat as he beheld the embodiment of the curse itself. "What is that?" Professor Mehta's voice shook with awe and dread. "It's the darkness incarnate, the malevolent force that has plagued Kaal Bhavan for centuries.

" The creature let out another earth-shaking roar, its eyes burning with hatred and malice. It lunged at them with unnatural speed, its claws slashing through the air like scythes. Rajiv and Professor Mehta scrambled to evade its attacks, their minds racing for a way to complete the ritual. With a surge of determination, Rajiv focused his mind on the incantations, blocking out the chaos around him. He chanted the final words of the ritual with unwavering resolve, each syllable resonating with ancient power. The creature recoiled, its form wavering and dissolving into tendrils of darkness.

The mansion trembled violently, as if the very fabric of reality were tearing apart. Rajiv felt a surge of energy rush through him, a surge of energy that seemed to pull him into the darkness. Suddenly, a blinding light filled the room, and Rajiv felt himself being lifted off the ground. He was surrounded by a swirling vortex of energy, pulling him toward a blinding white light. He could hear Professor Mehta's voice calling out to him, but it seemed distant and muffled.

As Rajiv emerged from the vortex, he found himself standing outside Kaal Bhavan, the mansion looming ominously behind him. The night air was crisp and cool, a stark contrast to the suffocating darkness he had just escaped. He turned to see Professor Mehta standing beside him, his expression one of awe and disbelief.

"We did it, Rajiv. We broke the curse.

" Rajiv nodded slowly, his mind still reeling from the ordeal. "But what about... Ananya?"

Professor Mehta's face fell, sorrow etched into his features.

"Her sacrifice won't be forgotten. She gave her life so that others could be free." As they stood in silence, a soft breeze swept through the air, carrying with it a sense of peace and closure.

The curse of Kaal Bhavan had been lifted, but the memories of their harrowing journey would linger with them forever. The first light of dawn painted the sky in hues of pink and gold, casting a gentle glow over the world. Rajiv and Professor Mehta watched as Kaal Bhavan stood silent and still, its dark secrets finally laid to rest.

www.ingramcontent.com/pod-product-compliance
Lightning Source LLC
Chambersburg PA
CBHW021754150726
47989CB00004B/1662